My First Picture Puzzles

Illustrated by Natasha Rimmington

Written by Moira Butterfield

Designed by Anton Poitier & Ben Potter

BARRON'S

First edition for the United States and Canada published in 2018 by
Barron's Educational Series, Inc.

Copyright © ISEEK Ltd 2017

All inquiries should be addressed to:
Barron's Educational Series, Inc.
250 Wireless Boulevard
Hauppauge, NY 11788
www.barronseduc.com

ISBN: 978-1-4380-1144-8

Date of Manufacture: June 2018
Manufactured by: Shenzhen Caimei Printing Co., Limited

Printed in China
9 8 7 6 5 4 3 2

Get puzzling!

This book has lots of fun picture puzzles. You'll need to look closely at the pictures to figure out the answers.

There are questions to answer on some of the pages too!

Toward the end of the book, some of the puzzles get a little harder. Don't worry if you get stuck with anything. The solutions are at the back of the book.

Use a pencil to write your answers to the questions. Have fun!

This tree is full of noisy parrots.
Draw a circle around the odd one out.

I found ☐ birds.

How many butterflies can you find hidden in the garden?

I found ☐ butterflies.

How many fish, starfish, and crabs can you count? Can you spot a shiny pearl?

☐ fish ☐ starfish ☐ crabs

Finish drawing faces on the funny people. How many hats are they wearing?

I counted ☐ hats.

Draw lines to connect the frogs that look the same.

What noise do frogs make? Frogs c_ _ _k.

Help the princess find her golden slippers.
Circle them when you spot them.

Give the princess a name. Princess [ ]

One pirate is captain of the ship, but which one? He has a blue hat and red boots.

Name the captain. Captain [   ]

These tigers all look the same, but some are different from the others!

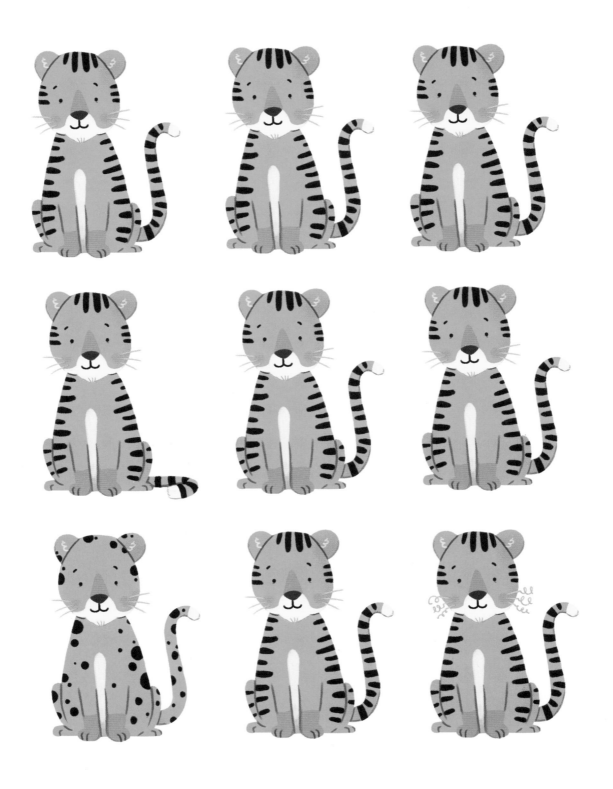

I found ☐ tigers that are different.

Which caterpillar ate the most leaves?

Check the right one. ☐ red ☐ blue

These leashes are all tangled!
Who owns the smallest dog?

The child with the g _ _ _ n shirt!

Draw lines to connect the animals and their shadows. How many animals are there?

I counted ⬚ animals.

How many naughty pigs like apples, hats, and getting muddy?

I found ☐ pigs that like all three things!

Draw lines to connect the moms and their babies. How many moms can you count?

I counted ☐ moms.

Which puzzle piece will fit the space?

A

B

C

Piece ☐ fits the space.

Welcome to the wildlife park! How many animals have trunks, stripes, and beaks?

☐ with trunks   ☐ with stripes   ☐ with beaks

Draw lines to connect the toys and the spaces where they belong.

Circle the toy that floats on water.

Help the skier get to her home. Which path should she take?

Can you find 3 owls hidden in the forest? Draw circles around them.

Help fix the robots.
Which piece belongs to which robot?

I counted [ ] buttons on each robot.

Connect the dots to find an animal in the desert.

I found a c_ _ _ _l.

The farmer needs to round up his sheep. Can you help him spot them all?

I found ☐ sheep.

Which way should the worm wiggle to avoid the hungry birds and reach the apple?

He chose the r_d line.

The spaceship is going to the planet BOING. Which one is it?

Planet ☐ is planet BOING.

Which bouquet has the most flowers?
Mark it with a check.

Connect the dots to draw the vases.

Help the rabbit get to her burrow and find four carrots on the way.

I counted ☐ carrots altogether.

Draw lines to connect the submarines that look the same. Find the odd one out.

I found ☐ submarines.

Draw a line to connect the right puzzle piece to each car.

I helped fix ☐ cars.

Draw lines connecting the cakes and the boxes they go in.

Draw your own yummy cake, too!

Can you spot something that doesn't fly?
Circle it.

I found ☐ birds.

Connect the dots to find a very big animal.

I found a d_____r.

How many people are riding bicycles?
How many buses are in the city?

| | bicycles | | buses |

Count the beetles and bees.

☐ beetles ☐ bees

Find all the things on the shopping list!
Circle them when you find them.

- ☐ bunny
- ☐ shoes
- ☐ piggy bank
- ☐ clock
- ☐ banana

Can you figure out the last color in each pattern? Color them in.

Can you find penguins hiding in the snow?

I found ☐ penguins.

Which horse is smallest? Circle it. Which horse is biggest? Mark it with a check. Which horse is ready to ride? Mark it with a star.

How many horses are there? ☐

Draw three more apples on the tree.

I counted ☐ apples.

Help the hikers reach the hilltop.

I counted ☐ birds on the hill.

Draw a line to the fairy's home.

My house has a chimney pipe and four windows.

This fairy is named _____.

Color in the circles to help the kitten find a path to its mommy.

How much does the food cost?
Draw a line to the right purse.

The drink costs 3 coins.
The box of eggs costs 5 coins.
The pie costs 7 coins.

I counted ☐ coins.

Draw a line from the right person to the right package.

Put an X by the plate with the most cherries. Put a check by the plate with the fewest cherries.

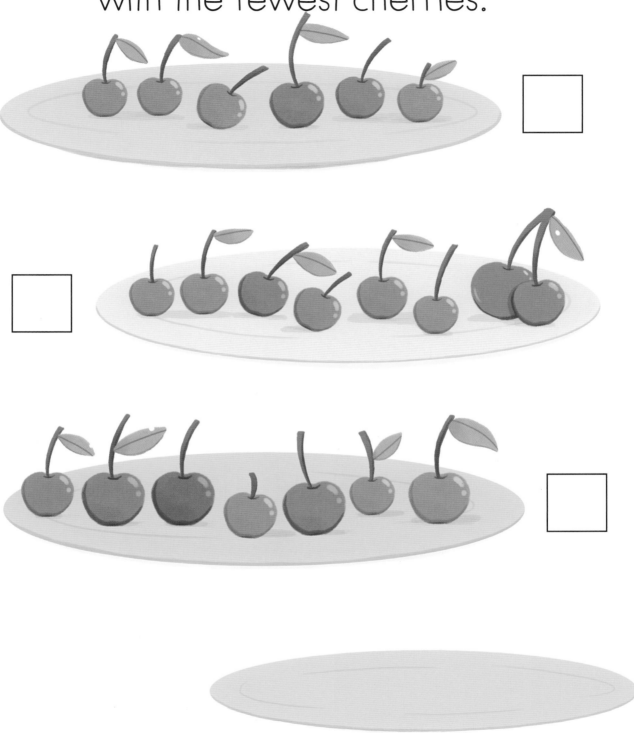

Draw something you like to eat on this plate.

Circle three things that are different in the bottom picture.

Finish drawing spots on the wriggly snakes.

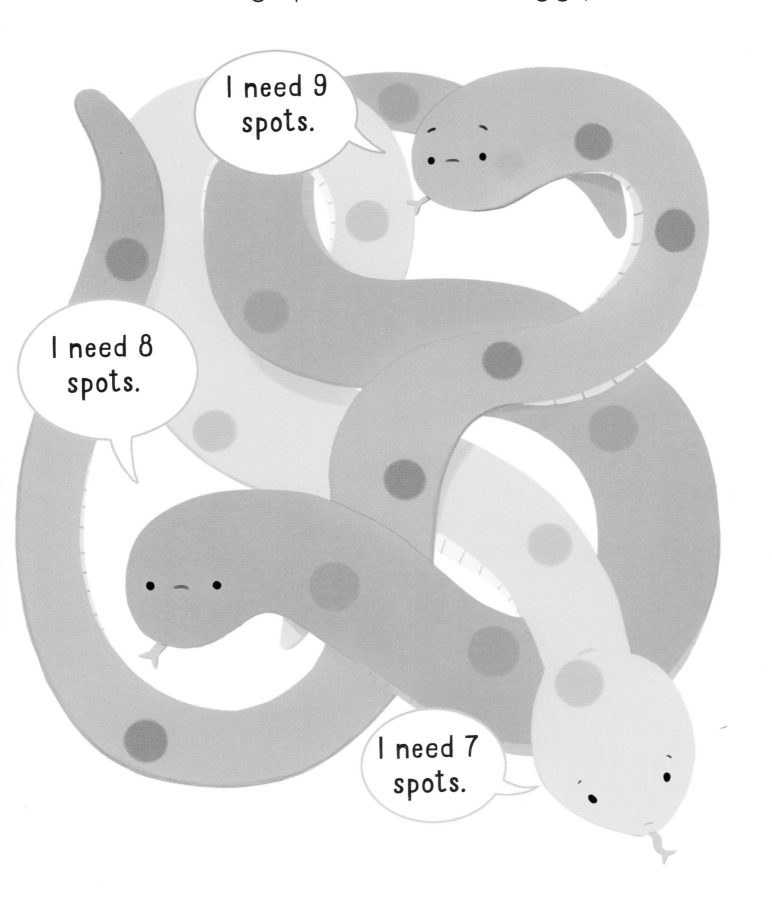

Circle three things that are different in the bottom picture.

Where should the dinosaur jigsaw pieces go?

I counted ☐ pieces.

Who is going where? Using different colored pencils, circle the people to match their planes.

☐ people are going on a sunny vacation.

Color in the diamonds to help the pirate find a treasure chest.

My treasure island is called _____ .

Connect the twins. Circle the child who doesn't have a twin.

How many balloons can you find?

I found ☐ balloons.

Can you help the children find their kites?

Draw lines connecting the children with their kites.

Draw a line to connect each animal mommy and baby. One has lost its mom.

Draw a mommy for the lonely baby.

The astronaut is going to a planet with rings and craters. Where did she go?

Mark the planet with an X.

Which flower has the most leaves?

Flower ☐ has the most leaves.

Which color should the frog follow to catch the bug?

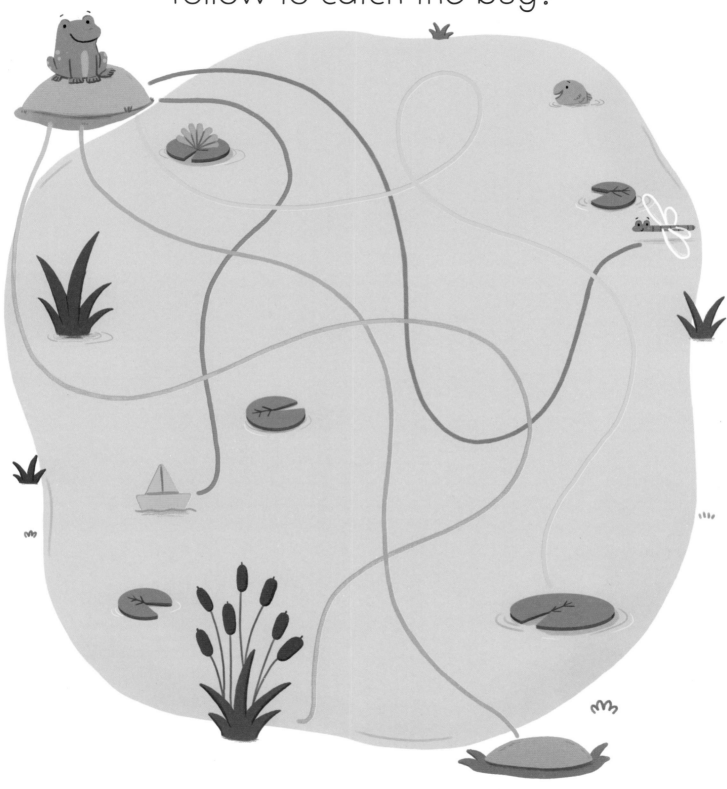

The frog follows the _____ line.

How many flying things can the children see?

They saw ☐ flying things.

7

7

1, 2, 3

5

croak

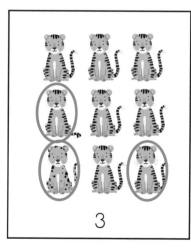

3

blue

green

6

3

4

c

2, 3, 4

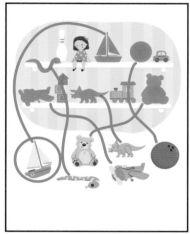

3

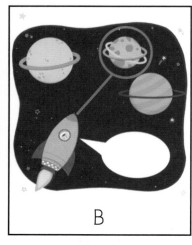

camel

9

red

B

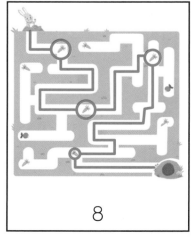

8

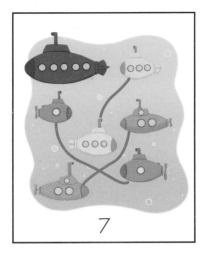

7

3

5

dinosaur

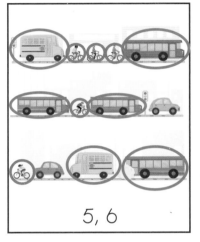

5, 6

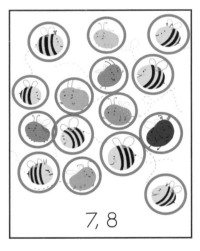

7, 8

9

7

8

10

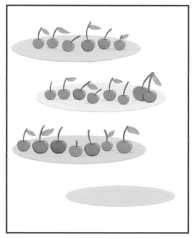

15

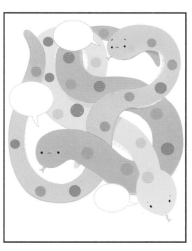

4

5

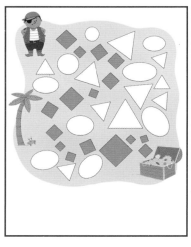

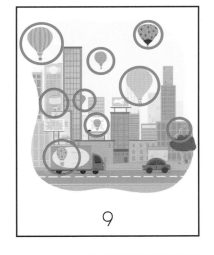

9

C

purple

6